ÉIRE NUA

A New Beginning

A Study of the
Irish Federal Solution
for
Peace, Dignity, and Prosperity
in a
Free and United Ireland

2012

Cumann Na Saoirse Náisiúnta
National Irish Freedom Committee

ISBN:978-1-300-36843-4

A Fenian Heritage Press production for National Irish Freedom Committee.

To aid scholars, bibliographic references are provided as footnotes sourcing each document.

Scholars wishing to study successive versions of Éire Nua, tracing the evolution of this dynamic program, can find the 1971 edition archived in the on line Irish Left Archive (http://cedarlounge.wordpress.com/archive-index/) and the 1979 edition archived on the CAIN website (http://cain.ulst.ac.uk/). The current version is available from Republican Sinn Féin, and is archived on their website (http://www.rsf.ie).

An extended table of contents, to facilitate study and quickly research selected topics, was developed especially for this edition.

This Book
is
dedicated
to those
in Ireland
and
throughout
the world
who continue
to build the
New Ireland

Table of Contents

Foreword

"Patriots of Ireland! Champions of Liberty in all lands. Be strong in hope. Your cause is identical with mine. You are calumniated in your day: I was misrepresented by the Loyalists of my day. Had I failed, the scaffold would have been my doom. But now my enemies do me honor...I stood true to my cause, even when victory had fled. In that I merited success. You must do likewise." - George Washington, Mt. Vernon, 1788

The histories of the United States and the Irish national struggle have always been closely intertwined. Much like the knot work of which the Irish artists are famous, the twists and turns of American – Irish politics are often complex and intricate. From the early Fenian American movement to President Clinton's lobbying on behalf of the ill-fated Good Friday Agreement, the United States' influence has played a changing but important role in Irish politics. Similarly, Irish men and women have risen to the call of defending their fellow Republic and adopted homeland throughout our nation's history. Ireland has given of her bosom many of her best scholars, statesmen, and soldiers to defend and spread the American ideals of freedom, equality, and justice for all. The time has come for Americans to take a new look at our foreign policy on Ireland; to consider the _New Ireland_ that we can help build, rather than sullenly mope at the failure of yet another status-quo solution.

The early history of the Irish in America is rather thoroughly documented in Condon's "_The Irish Race in America_" and more recently in the pioneering work of Derek Warfield of the Young Wolfe Tones. Expansive as it is, the Irish influence in America is too deep a topic to cover in such a brief introduction. We will focus instead specifically on Irish-American political action within the last fifty years.

In 1973, Irish-American activist Fred Burns O'Brien succeeded in having a summary of the Éire Nua peace plan entered into the Congressional Record. The introduction by sponsor Rep. Tip O' Neill referred to it as, "a solution to the present situation in Northern Ireland which merits consideration". At the same time in Ireland, proponents of Éire Nua were already actively holding organizational and informative meetings across sectarian lines. Influential in this process in Ireland were the noted author Desmond Fennell and Bronx entrepreneur Emmett O'Connell. Both toured and wrote extensively promoting the Éire Nua peace plan[1].

Indeed, the present authors are deeply indebted, particularly, to Mr. Fennell's pioneering work, "*Sketches of the New Ireland*" which lays out a methodology and preliminary analysis of the structures within the New Ireland.

In 1978, then-Chairman of the House Judiciary Rep. Peter Rodino (along with Rep. Joshua Eilberg and Rep. Hamilton Fish IV), commissioned a fact-finding delegation to Ireland to investigate U.S. State Department collusion in the denial of visas to individuals advocating alternative solutions to the Irish conflict. Notable among those denied visas was Ruairí Ó Brádaigh, a co-author of the Éire Nua peace plan. The resulting document, "*Justice Report - Politics and Visa Denials*" expressed the team's belief that corruption and political pressure were widely used to wrongly suppress voices of dissent.

In Ireland, support for Éire Nua was growing exponentially, with prominent Unionists as well as Nationalists endorsing the program. A steady stream of explanatory and expository material was generated to meet the public demand for knowledge of this unique Irish proposal. Indeed, history has revealed that even the British were seriously considering withdrawal as an option.

Always eager to snatch defeat from the jaws of victory, corrupt elements in the northern Provisional Sinn Féin leadership abandoned Éire Nua. Using resources

---

1 See "Bibliography & Suggested Reading" for a representative list

gathered through legitimate political activities and business, as well as corruption and intimidation, and aided by a willing (and unwilling) media blackout, the Éire Nua program was successfully buried.

Thus, when President Clinton undertook once again to help bring peace to our beloved friend Ireland, he was repeatedly mislead to believe that no other alternative existed other than the Good Friday Agreement. Substantively differing very little from prior failed arrangements (such as the Sunningdale Agreement), the GFA was actively promoted as the only peace plan possible for Ireland. After significant lobbying and effort on the part of President Clinton and others, two separate votes were held in Ireland. Spurious claims that the positive vote for the GFA represented the true needs and desires of all Ireland were made, but fell apart on examination. In the 26-county state, a poorly attended referendum resulted in barely over 50% of the population even bothering to vote. Only in the 6-county statelet would anyone dare call a vote held under the auspices of an occupying military as well as armed paramilitary gangs (all with a stake in the outcome) as being fair and representative.

Fourteen years on, we see the failure of the GFA in ever increasing spirals of sectarian violence and economic collapse. Still the lie is spread that there is no alternative. Éire Nua activists organized by Cumann na Saoirse Náisiúnta have kept the flame alive, however, including a historic 2010 visit to DC by Brian Wardlow, and a 2012 visit by Mike Costello of CnSN and Mary Ward of Republican Sinn Féin to launch the new Éire Nua awareness pamphlet, "Éire Nua – Peace, Dignity, & Prosperity in a United Ireland". However much progress the pamphlet generated, what was needed was a concise *handbook* of information for both the activist as well as the interested reader.

For this reason, we have collected, updated, and expanded the existing materials produced by supporters of the Éire Nua program in the United States. It is our sincere hope that by producing this volume we can add to the discussion of both the Irish struggle and U.S. Foreign policy in regards to Irish independence. We consider it an honor to be able to offer our humble contribution towards a lasting peace with justice in the New Ireland.

Seosamh Flaithbheartaigh
Cumann na Saoirse Náisiúnta
Chairman, Éire Nua Committee

Dominick Bruno Jr.
Fenian Heritage Press
Editor

Introduction[2]

The Treaty of 1921 that partitioned Ireland into two sectarian statelets was, at worst, a betrayal of Irish aspirations and, at best, a temporary solution to avoid an all-out war, as claimed by its signatories and supporters. After nearly a century of political and economic chaos, it is obvious that the Treaty was flawed, and is in fact the root cause of the ongoing war. Therefore, it is now time to repeal the Treaty and replace it with a new agreement wherein the British would concede Irish sovereignty, thus clearing the way for the Irish people of both traditions to unite in one free and independent nation.

To this end, we are proposing the establishment of a Constituent Assembly as a first step in the process. The proposed Assembly would draft a new 32-county all-Ireland Constitution that would:

1. establish political and popular sovereignty for the protection of human rights and social justice,

2. establish a new government structure based on a federation of the four historic provinces of Ireland, and

3. establish an independent judiciary.

The second step in this process would be a British declaration of intent to withdraw from Ireland based on the above agreement. The final step would be the release of all political prisoners.

---

2 This section is comprised of 3 essays, "The First Step Towards A Peaceful Ireland" *(Éire Nua Newsletter, Volume 1, #3, June 1993),* "The Second Step Towards A Peaceful Ireland" *(Éire Nua Newsletter, Volume Volume 1, #4, September 1993),* & "The Third Step Towards A Peaceful Ireland" *(Éire Nua Newsletter, Volume 1, #5, December 1992)*

The convening of a Constituent Assembly is a logical first step in a process designed to bring peace, unity, and prosperity to Ireland. It offers the prospect of a permanent solution, as opposed to the failed Sunningdale, Hillsborough, and Brooke-type initiatives put forward by the British and Dublin governments. This proposal is not new, nor is it radical. It is, in fact, similar in may respects to the 1787 Constitutional Convention convened in Philadelphia to draft a new federal constitution for the emerging United States of America.

Since that time, many other emerging nations came into existence through a similar process. A prime present-day example is South Africa, a country where the vast majority of its people have been enslaved by a descendant colonist minority. Many felt this situation would never change, but South Africa today is a country in transition[3].

The road towards a peaceful Ireland is fraught with obstacles, inherent and protected in the political and economic status quo. In this climate, any proposal guaranteeing equal rights and opportunity to all the people of Ireland is not welcome. The initiatives put forward by the British and Dublin governments are minor revisions to the Treaty of 1921, primarily intended to perpetuate the status quo, and therefore destined to end in failure.

The proposed Constituent Assembly would be representative of the whole people of Ireland and would be elected by the suffrage of the adult population. The Assembly's sole function would be to draft a new Constitution. The draft Constitution would then be submitted to the people in referendum for acceptance or rejection. This open democratic process would be more

---

3 The example of Iceland 2010-2012 shows a similar course of action by patriotic citizens to restructure their government. See *Washington Times,* 12 January 2012 "Iceland makes fledgling recovery from its economic meltdown".

meaningful to the Irish people today than the closed-door meetings held between the same politicians who have failed the people so often in the past. All elements of Irish society would be free to contest the election for the Assembly. This approach would ensure that the relations of the Irish people with each other and with the world at large would be determined through free and open debate.

In order for this process to succeed, all politicians and political parties expressing an interest in or concern for Ireland's future must put aside their differences and participate for the common good. In addition, all those individuals and political parties now excluded must be included in the process and allowed access to the media. If for no other reason, the Irish people deserve the opportunity to participate in such a process.

The Conquest of Ireland and the need for British Withdrawal

The conquest of Ireland was gradual, taking over 130 years to accomplish. In fact, the Norman invasion of eight hundred years ago was not a conquest in the true sense of the word, for it conquered only land. It failed miserably to pacify and conquer the people. After centuries of occupation and institutionalized pogroms including dispossession, famine, religious persecution, forced emigration, and internment, England is still trying to pacify the Irish people and hold sway over their lives.

It appears that the liberation of Ireland is destined to be a slow process, as was its conquest. What started almost a century ago with the 1916 Easter Rising is an ongoing process that will in time rid Ireland of the last vestiges of colonialism. Until this process runs its course, Ireland will remain a troubled land, divided, and possessed of a *terrible beauty*.

The rise of an empire, whether it be Roman, Ottoman, or British, brings to its human victims humiliation, pain and, death and to its captive nations plunder, division, and shame. It thrives on ignorance and fear and survives on the spoils of war. The decline of an empire, however welcome, brings with it a renewed ferocity. Its armies are set loose on the general populace in a desperate effort to survive by intimidation. Such is the situation in Ireland today. The British army is on the rampage, but its days in Ireland are numbered.

That same army serves as the enforcer of British rule in Ireland and is therefore a symbol of domination. This symbol must be removed before the divided people of Ireland can get back together to decide what is best for them.

On Nov. 9th 1990, Peter Brooke, the British government Minister in occupied Ireland, stated that Britain has no selfish, strategic, or economic interest in staying in Ireland. If this be so, then let them state publicly their intent to withdraw politically and militarily from Ireland.

In order to effect such a withdrawal, the British government must be willing to negotiate an agreement that incorporates the following provisions:

1. a commitment to withdraw from Ireland after the Irish people have adopted a new Constitution,

2. a cessation of hostilities coupled with a return to barracks of all military personnel,

3. a commitment to remove all its military hardware from Ireland, and

4. a commitment to refrain from arming pro-British paramilitary organizations during the withdrawal process.

These conditions of withdrawal are general in nature and represent only the views of the authors. They do not presume to, nor do they, represent the views or negotiating strategy of any party or individual who may be involved in future negotiations involving a British withdrawal.

There are many other factors that will come into play and must be dealt with once a British declaration of intent to withdraw is secured. For instance, a territorial army will be assembled to replace the security forces of the two existing states. A new criminal justice system will be established to replace the existing politicized system whose stock in trade includes special police units, interrogation centers, military tribunals, non-jury courts, internment camps, and political prisoners.

In order to create a new criminal justice system, the police forces of the existing two states will be restructured into regional police forces controlled by and accountable to regional authorities. Similarly, the existing judicial system that now includes military tribunals and non-jury courts will be replaced with an independent judicial system that will operate within the framework and constraints of the new all-Ireland Constitution. Political prisons, interrogation centers and internment camps will be closed down for there will be no political dissenters tortured or imprisoned in the new Ireland.

Political Prisoners & the Need for Justice

For eight centuries the people of Ireland have struggled for the right to be masters in their own country. England the Oppressor has been ruthless in exerting and maintaining its control over Ireland and its people. It is difficult to appreciate why she still maintains such a policy, especially now that colonialism has outlived its usefulness, however dubious that may been in the first place. It is even more difficult to understand England's willingness to use draconian laws, torture, prison camps, and military force to enforce this policy. Generally, a government of intelligent, clear-thinking individuals would abandon such a policy, especially one that has not worked in eight hundred years. But insofar as Ireland is concerned, England is paralyzed in a political paradigm that filters out reality, thus leaving herself and Ireland victims of history.

Pope Paul II in addressing the Polish people said, *"People have a right and even a duty to protect their existence against an unjust aggressor. Christians may have no hesitation that in the name of elementary justice, proportionate means may be used against an unjust aggressor. There can be no peace in a society that does not respect the rights of the individual."*

Speaking at Auschwitz the Pope said,

"But the memory of even one should be a warning sign on the part of humanity today, in order that every kind of concentration camp anywhere on earth may once and for all be done away with. And everything recalls that horrible experience should also disappear forever, from the lives of nations and states, everything that is a continuation of these experiences under different forms, namely the various kinds of torture and oppression either physical or moral, carried out under any system in any land. This phenomenon is all the more distressing if it occurs under the pretext of internal security or the need to preserve an apparent peace."

Any reasonable person can take the words of the Pope and apply them to the Irish situation. In both parts of Ireland, in England, Scotland, and Wales, there are hundreds of men and women imprisoned and routinely tortured as a direct consequence of England's continued presence in Ireland. Proof of torture has been well documented by the European Court of Human Rights and by Amnesty International on numerous occasions. Further proof of inhuman treatment can be found by examining the cases of the Birmingham Six, the Guilford Four, and the Maguire family. All were falsely accused and tortured until they confessed to crimes they did not commit. They were then convicted on the weight of the forced confessions and fabricated forensic evidence. Combined, they served over two hundred years in prison. All of these convictions have since been found to be flawed and overturned on appeal.

As one of the conditions to any settlement leading towards a peaceful Ireland, the status of all prisoners must be reviewed and resolved. Those imprisoned in Ireland, England, Scotland, and Wales for purely political reasons must be freed unconditionally. For those imprisoned in other countries, a representation would be made for their release as a gesture of goodwill and friendship. The other category of prisoner is those who engaged in sectarian killings, or who deliberately chose innocent civilians as their primary target. Because of the nature of such acts, these cases would be subjected to independent judicial review to determine their status. All prisoners irrespective of their political affiliation would be granted the same treatment under this process. The conditions set forth in this book for the treatment of political prisoners represents only the views of the authors. They do not presume to, nor do they, represent the views or negotiating strategy of any party or individual who may be involved in future negotiations involving the release of political prisoners.

History[4]

In the mid-sixties, Dáithí Ó Conaill, the author of
Éire Nua, was involved with a very successful local co-
operative venture in County Donegal. The co-operative was
located in a remote, economically depressed and neglected
area, plagued by emigration and unemployment. Working
with Fr. McDyer, the founder of the co-operative concept,
Dáithí realized that local people, when given the
opportunity and direction, could manage and improve the
local economy, stem the flow of emigration, and improve
the quality of their own lives.

During his involvement with the venture, Dáithí also
realized that the physical remoteness of the local people
from the center of power in Dublin was directly related to
the neglect and hardship suffered by them. This condition
was further exacerbated by the psychological barrier created
by their forced separation from their neighbors in the six
counties of Ulster occupied by the British. The experience
of directing, working with, and observing local people
succeed in managing their own affairs, independent of
central authority, had a profound effect on Dáithí and was
responsible for planting the seeds of the Éire Nua concept
in his mind. Nurtured by his political ability and his desire
to plan for the future, the seeds took root and blossomed
into the concept of a new beginning not just for Donegal
and Ulster but also for all of Ireland.

---

4 Originally serialized in _Éire Nua Newsletter,_ beginning with _Volume 1, #3_ and
continuing through _Volume 3, #1._

Dáithí realized that the first step in creating a new Ireland was the reunification of the nine-county province of Ulster. In expounding on this concept in 1969, he wrote:

"By creating a provincial parliament for the nine counties of Ulster, within the framework of a new Ireland the partition system would be disestablished and the problem of the border removed. The Protestant people of Ulster would have a working majority and would have immediate access to power. Furthermore, the devolution of power to the local level would ensure for each community the opportunity to foster its own traditions and culture. Each region and community would have within itself the immediate power to deal with its own social and economic problems. Such devolution of power from one central authority to the people is the essence of democracy. The Nationalist population would be of sufficient strength to ensure a strong and credible opposition within reach of power. For the first time in fifty years we would see a normalization of politics with an end to the domination of one community by another and the resultant frustration and conflict."

In 1969, when war broke out again in Ireland, Dáithí was deeply involved with the Republican movement. Prior to the onset of internment in August 1971 he presented his ideas of Éire Nua to the Republican leadership and was subsequently given the green light to proceed. On the 21st of August 1971 at the West Ernan Hotel in Monaghan, with over 500 people anxiously waiting outside in the square, the Leadership of Provisional Sinn Féin publicly announced the Éire Nua program. Historians, local and foreign media and prominent people including Sinn Féin delegates from all over Ireland enthusiastically greeted the birth of Éire Nua.

The Launching of Éire Nua

In 1967, while Dáithí Ó Connaill was putting the finishing touches to Éire Nua, an unrelated movement was coming to the forefront in the occupied six counties of northeast Ireland. The non-violent civil rights movement inspired by Martin Luther King, Jr. took to the streets demanding equality in employment, housing, voting rights, police, and civil rights. These demonstrations were met with violent opposition from Stormont, the Northern Ireland Government. They were attacked and beaten by Unionists mobs led by the police (RUC) and B Specials (militia). Their homes and communities were burned to the ground, many were killed and thousands were forced to flee across the border to the 26-County State.

One of the most significant marches of this period took place from Derry to Belfast. Bernadette Devlin, a student activist, led it. The marchers were set upon by a frenzied mob of Unionists led by the RUC and B-Specials. This was the first time that the outside world saw the true nature of the Northern Ireland State. The Republican movement was not initially involved in events of this period. However, as the state-led violence escalated against the Nationalists, the IRA was asked for help in defending the communities against the Unionist onslaught. During this same period, while thousands were fleeing across the border, the 26-County State, notwithstanding its promise of "not standing idly by", did in fact stand by and let the onslaught happen. Meanwhile the IRA, acting in a defensive role, was successful in securing the Nationalist areas.

In the meantime, the British Government poured tens of thousands of troops into the north under the pretext of defending the Nationalist communities against the Unionist mobs. However, the role of the British army soon became evident when they ceased playing the role of "peacemaker" and were instead deployed as "security forces" in Nationalist areas. To counter the successes of the IRA in defending these areas, the Stormont Government, on August 9th 1971, with the help of the British army introduced internment without trial. The victims of this pogrom were all taken from Nationalist areas.

During this period the civil rights movement became radicalized as a result of the treatment they received at the hands of the Stormont government. They participated in acts of civil disobedience including anti-internment protest demonstrations. It was on one such demonstration in Derry on Sunday, January 30th 1972 that British paratroopers opened fire, killing thirteen instantly and wounding scores of others. This murder of unarmed demonstrators became known as the Bloody Sunday massacre and in effect signaled the end of peaceful protests and the beginning of war.

Aware of the consequences of the approaching war, the Army Council of the IRA endorsed Dáithí Ó Connaill's plan for a political solution for Ireland. On August IIth 1971, two days after internment, they issued a statement calling for the setting-up of an alternative form of government for Ulster.

The Promotion of Éire Nua

The statement of August 11th 1971, calling for an alternative form of government for the nine counties of Ulster, was the official launching of Éire Nua. One week later on August 18th, Ruairí Ó Brádaigh, President of Sinn Féin, issued a statement endorsing the proposals. The statement said that the people of Ulster should proceed to set up a Regional Parliament for the nine counties of Ulster.

It continued by saying that the settlement of 1921 that set up both the Stormont and Dublin parliaments was unworkable and against the interests of the Irish people. It called for the dismantling of both statelets to make room for the New Ireland. It concluded by calling on the people of Connacht to consider joining Ulster in setting up their own Regional Parliament.

On August 21st 1971, a convention was assembled in Monaghan to consider the establishment of an Ulster Parliament (Dáil Uladh). Invitations were sent to a broad spectrum of people including elected officials representing various political viewpoints. All nine counties of Ulster were represented. This convention drew both national and international attention and received major media coverage. Amongst those attending were two Westminster parliamentarians, Frank McManus and Paddy Kennedy. Since these were the only parliamentary level officials present, it was decided that as a first step a council would be set up to promote Dáil Uladh. Paddy Kennedy and Frank McManus were selected to head up the council. Aided by a constitutional expert from Dublin the council drafted structures for local and provincial governments.

The next meeting of major significance was held in Tuam, the old capital of Connacht. Desmond Fennell and Maura Conlon organized the meeting. Various organizations and individuals attended from all five counties of Connacht. This meeting drew national attention and received major media coverage, as did the meeting in Monaghan. A council was set up for the same purpose as was the council in Ulster and Officers were elected to head it up. Follow-up meetings were held in Tuam, Westport and Drumshambo.

In the spring of 1972, a committee was formed at University College Galway to study the implications of and make recommendations for setting up a federal system consisting of the four provinces. The main question considered was whether Éire Nua was to be set up as a unitary system with regional assemblies or a federal republic with four provincial parliaments. The basic difference highlighted by the committee was that a regional assembly could be suspended at will by the central government, as was Stormont by the British government. On the other hand, in a federal arrangement there would be a sharing of powers between the provinces and the center. In this situation the Federal government could not suspend the provincial parliament. The Supreme Court would be the final arbiter in all disputes between the provinces and the center. The latter arrangement was selected by the Leadership of the Republican Movement and is today the basis for the Éire Nua program.

Growing Resistance to Éire Nua

The suspension of the Stormont government by the British government in the spring of 1972 created a political vacuum. It provided a realistic opportunity for the political parties in Ireland to put forward their solutions to achieve a permanent peace for the Irish people. The Irish Republican movement stepped into the breach and continued to politicize the Éire Nua program. A further obstacle was removed when on June 28th 1972 a bilateral truce was called between the IRA and the British government. However, the Dublin government and the various political parties who had paid lip service to Irish unity remained silent and instead resorted to undermining negotiations for peace.

On June 28th 1972 a press conference was held at the Ormond Hotel in Dublin to promote the Éire Nua program. The program was based on the formation of four Provincial Parliaments with a federal Parliament at the center. Media representatives attended the press conference from Ireland, Britain and the rest of Europe. Despite attempts to sidetrack the main issue, the Irish Republican representatives managed to highlight their proposal for a new Ireland. They emphasized that their proposals were not definitive or exclusive of other proposals. They also stated that the European Convention for the Protection of Human Rights and Fundamental Freedom would be incorporated in the domestic law of the new Ireland and indicated that the new Ireland would be a complete break with the past.

Due to the ongoing success and growing interest in the Éire Nua program, the Dublin government became fearful of its own position of privilege and power and acted against the Republican movement by banning Sinn Féin spokespersons from radio and television. The result was that while the BBC, UTV, and other major European networks carried the press conference live, Irish radio and television downplayed the event, thus depriving the Irish people of the opportunity to judge for themselves the merits of the Éire Nua program. Gradually, the noose of censorship was tightened and in 1976, Conor Cruise O'Brien made censorship official government policy.

The media in the United States also applied censorship when on a coast-to-coast television discussion among Unionists, Nationalists, and Republicans, broadcast from Boston, John Hume advocated and managed to have Ruairí Ó Brádaigh's Éire Nua proposals deleted from the program. However, on returning to Ireland, Ó Brádaigh stated that during a chance meeting with Mr. Gerry L'Estrange, a member of the 26-County Parliament, who declared that "nobody could take away from your regional government policy, it is very progressive"

Unionist Reaction to Éire Nua

During the bilateral talks between the IRA and the British government in 1972, the late Dáithí Ó Conaill presented William Whitelaw with a copy of the Éire Nua program. This action by Ó Conaill left no doubt as to whether or not the British government was aware of the Irish Republican Movement's intent regarding the Irish question. However, they refused to give the Movement credit for having put forward a sound political solution to the Irish question. The talks themselves ended in failure.

Despite official censorship in the 26-county state, a Council was successfully set up in Munster to promote Dáil Mumhan followed by a similar Council in Leinster. In 1973, a Council of Ireland was launched and a number of meetings were held in Athlone to promote the program. Representatives from the four provinces attended the Athlone meetings. During the same period a number of meetings were held throughout Ireland where leaders of the Republican movement discussed the Éire Nua policy with prominent members of the pro-British Loyalist and Unionist parties.

At a seminar held in Galway in 1974, Frank McManus M.P. speaking of Éire Nua, stated "there was nothing as powerful as an idea whose time has come" and "the only criticism that can be made of Éire Nua, was the source from where it came and that was not a valid criticism"

In the summer of 1974, during the taping of a UTV talk show, Sammy Smith of the UDA expressed his concern to Ruairí Ó Brádaigh about the changing population (the lower ratio of Protestants to Catholics) in a nine-county new Ulster. Such a comment by a hard-line Loyalist leader, albeit negative, represented fresh thinking on the part of some leaders of the ultra hard-line Loyalist community. More discussions took place with the Rev. Eric Gallagher, a leading Methodist Minister, who stated that political scientists in leading universities had analyzed Éire Nua and found no fault with its systems of checks and balances.

In 1976, the Rev. Billy Arklow, who later became Dean of St. Andrews Cathedral in Belfast, arranged for Ó Brádaigh to make a twenty-minute presentation of Éire Nua at Queen's University in Belfast, to an assemblage that included leaders of the Protestant community. The presentation was well received as demonstrated by the number and types of questions asked. Harry Murray, Chairman of the Ulster Workers Council, had commented that the Éire Nua program was similar to the Australian system, which is a federation of states that seemed to work well.

The Undermining of Éire Nua

The steady growth of Éire Nua in the mid-seventies was led by the Irish Republican Movement and endorsed by the IRA. This did not deter pro-British Loyalists and Unionists from becoming involved in direct discussions on the Éire Nua federal policy with leading Irish Republicans, most notably the late Dáithí Ó Conaill and Ruairí Ó Brádaigh.

In 1974, Desmond Boal added his voice to the growing Loyalist opinion favoring Éire Nua. Boal, who was secretary to Ian Paisley, published a statement favoring a two-state federal solution, comprising the 26-county and the 6-county states. While the Republican leadership

16

realized that it was a major step forward to have Loyalists and Unionists come out in favor of British disengagement and a federal solution of sorts, they felt that the two-state federation would not work as they would be eternally at loggerheads, i.e. Czechoslovakia. However, discussions continued with Boal and others until the collapse of the Power Sharing Executive.

The large number of publications of that era indicates that the Irish people recognized that there was a solution and that the Éire Nua federal policy was their first choice. Amongst the most prominent publications were, _Towards a Greater Ulster_, _Ireland as a Whole_, _Take the Faeroes for Example_, _The Third Republic_, _A New Nationalism_ - Desmond Fennell; _Ulster the Future_ - Frank McManus M.P.; _Shaping a New Society_ - Emmet O'Connell; _Our People our Future_ - Ruairí Ó Brádaigh[5].

However, there were undercurrents developing within the Irish Republican Movement due to the influx of newcomers, especially in the North. Emerging from these would be the men and women who would lead the blanket protest and give their lives on hunger strike and wage an all-out war for a united Ireland. However, there were also those with personal agendas who viewed the situation as an opportune moment to take control of the Irish Republican movement. These opportunists, aware that the Republican leadership of the day was highly respected because of Éire Nua, campaigned for their gradual removal by undermining Éire Nua.

At the 1980 Sinn Féin Ard-Fheis the Belfast leadership, along with branches in Dublin, moved to have the term federalism removed from Sinn Féin policy and replaced with the term maximum decentralization. Dáithí Ó

---

5 For these and others, see the "Bibliography & Suggested Reading"

Conaill later resigned from Sinn Féin, having become the first victim of political cleansing. Dáithí later returned as Vice-President of the newly formed Republican Sinn Féin and authored "*Towards a Peaceful Ireland*" and "*Éire Nua - A New Democracy*", the updated version of Éire Nua, prior to his untimely death in 1991._

The Rebirth of Éire Nua

To recap, the late Dáithí Ó Conaill, one of the leading military strategists and political visionaries of seventies, founded Éire Nua. Along with Ruairí Ó Brádaigh, President of Republican Sinn Féin, Dáithí opened a dialogue with leaders of Loyalist groups in the occupied six counties. Many meetings were held during the Éire Nua promotional campaign of the seventies, but personal ambitions within the Republican movement and opposition from the proponents of the status quo seemed to have buried Éire Nua. In the meantime, we have been dealt initiatives, super initiatives, and now hyper initiatives by the governments in London and Dublin.

The saying that nothing good comes easy can be applied to Éire Nua as it makes a slow comeback, spearheaded by Republican Sinn Féin in Ireland. Again we see a growing awareness of Éire Nua, manifested by more meetings and media attention. Since then a number of significant events have attested to its rebirth. On December 7th, 1993 a press conference was held in Belfast to launch the new bilingual Éire Nua program. At the press conference, Ruairí Ó Brádaigh, in a message to the Unionists, said: "that in the context of an English public undertaking to withdraw, the Ulster identity is a legitimate identity which can find expression in a nine-county Ulster parliament with strong local government. The position of each of the four provinces would be entrenched in a new Federal Ireland in a written constitution with complete separation of church and state and a pluralist society." Channel Four and Sky news in Britain reports covered the press conference, as did the Irish Times and Belfast Telegraph.

In June of 2000, Bertie Ahern, the 26-county Prime Minister 'damned the Éire Nua program with faint praise' by stating that while Éire Nua had its merits those who promoted it, i.e. Republican Sinn Féin, were suspect because they did not engage in the 'peace process'. Ruairí Ó Brádaigh replied by stating that the British had no problem sitting down to discuss the Éire Nua peace plan at the height of the war in the 70's.

The NIFC Endorses Éire Nua

Since its founding in 1987, the National Irish Freedom Committee (NIFC) has endorsed the Éire Nua program and has been promoting it in the United States ever since. The NIFC views Éire Nua as a comprehensive Irish formula for a just and lasting peace in Ireland. This program is in stark contrast to British sponsored 'peace initiatives', such as the Anglo-Irish Treaty of 1921, Sunningdale, Hillsborough, and the Good Friday Agreement, all designed to copper-fasten and legitimize British control over the occupied six counties of Ireland.

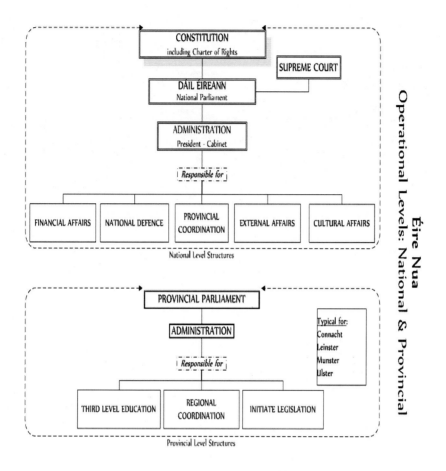

Organizational chart reflecting the flow of responsibility on the National and Provincial level under the proposed federal program, Éire Nua.

For a detailed explanation, see the following chapter.

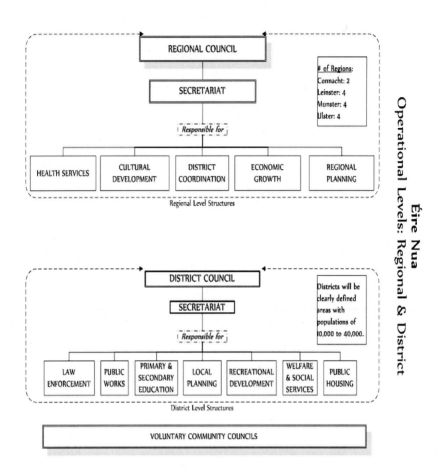

REGIONAL COUNCIL

SECRETARIAT

# of Regions:
Connacht: 2
Leinster: 4
Munster: 4
Ulster: 4

Responsible for

| HEALTH SERVICES | CULTURAL DEVELOPMENT | DISTRICT COORDINATION | ECONOMIC GROWTH | REGIONAL PLANNING |

Regional Level Structures

DISTRICT COUNCIL

SECRETARIAT

Districts will be clearly defined areas with populations of 10,000 to 40,000.

Responsible for

| LAW ENFORCEMENT | PUBLIC WORKS | PRIMARY & SECONDARY EDUCATION | LOCAL PLANNING | RECREATIONAL DEVELOPMENT | WELFARE & SOCIAL SERVICES | PUBLIC HOUSING |

District Level Structures

VOLUNTARY COMMUNITY COUNCILS

Organizational chart reflecting the flow of responsibility on the Regional and District level under the proposed federal program, Éire Nua.

For a detailed explanation, see the following chapter.

Fundamental Principles[6]

The concept on which Éire Nua is based, that of a unitary federation of the four historic provinces under the coordination of a national parliament, would foster a true democracy and eliminate the causes for conflict, such as Ireland has experienced for the past eight hundred years. The Éire Nua constitution with its Charter of Rights would guarantee all of Ireland's people true freedom, a home for its children and a new beginning.

The Constitution as envisioned in the Éire Nua program would embody the intent of the 1916 Proclamation as well as the following fundamental principles:

1. a Charter of Rights,

2. Separation of Church and State,

3. an independent Judicial System, and

4. new Government Structures.

The first fundamental principle, a Charter of Rights, would be based on the premise that recognizes the fundamental dignity and importance of the individual, who at birth is endowed with a basic right to be treated as a unique and inviolable human being. Based on this premise the Charter of Rights would guarantee the right to life, liberty, and security of person. It would also guarantee the

---

6 The texts comprising this chapter were first serialized in *Éire Nua Newsletter*, *Vol. 2, #2* through *Vol.3 #2*, as "A Look at the New Constitution", "A Look at the Éire Nua Government National Level", "A Look at the Éire Nua Government Provincial Level", & "A Look at the Éire Nua Government Regional Level".

23

rights of citizenship, civil rights, property rights, equal rights, workers rights, and equal protection under the law. It would prohibit the government from granting unto itself special powers that can be used against the people.

The second fundamental principle, Separation of Church and State, would prohibit the government from supporting, promoting, or granting special status to any religion over another or to any individual over another because of religious beliefs or affiliations. It would guarantee the right to hold any or no religious belief without prejudice in either the public or private arena. It would also guarantee that religious morality is not legislated to the detriment of nonconformists or others with differing values.

The third fundamental principle, an Independent Judicial System, would guarantee judicial safeguards including the power of judicial review. The Supreme Court, in its role as head of an independent judicial system and guardian of the Constitution, would ensure that the government cannot circumvent the Constitution, the supreme law of the land, for political or any other reason. The second most important role of an independent Judiciary would be to ensure that a court of law remains a neutral arena in which the protagonists, the accused, and the accuser can argue before an impartial arbiter, and that the verdict is based on all of the evidence and rendered by a jury of peers.

The fourth fundamental principle, New Government Structures, would be based on a federation of the four provinces under the coordination of a national parliament with powers devolved through regional administrative councils to local bodies so that at all levels citizens may have an effective voice in their own governance. All levels of government would receive their powers from the people, whose representatives would be elected by the suffrage of the adult population. The national parliament would be the supreme authority in exercising those powers solely delegated to it by the Constitution.

A Charter of Rights

Many countries that subscribe to the Universal Declaration of Human Rights interpret its meaning in narrow self-serving terms. According to reports published by Amnesty International, Helsinki Watch, Asia Watch, and the US State Department, approximately one third of the U.N. member states are guilty, to varying degrees, of human rights abuses. One would not expect England and Ireland to fall into this category. Unfortunately, they do, as both have enacted laws that contravene provisions of the European Court for the Protection of Fundamental Rights and Freedom[7]. A review of the repressive laws enacted by both governments show a remarkable similarity in content and timing. It appears as if their efforts were coordinated and directed against those who would challenge or attempt to change the immoral partition of Ireland. It's estimated that close to one million people in both England and Ireland have been victims of these repressive laws.

The political leaders of the eviscerated 6-county administration, realizing that their only hope of maintaining control over the rump state was by repressive means, enacted as their first piece of legislation the infamous Special Powers Act of 1922. This draconian piece of legislation gave the police extreme powers to arrest without warrant, and incarcerate without trial, any Catholic they classified as a "political suspect". In 1973 the Special

7 Indeed, the United States' own Public Law 107-56, the USA PATRIOT Act, contravenes a number of provisions of the European Court.

Powers Act was repeated and replaced by the Emergency Act. This Act retained most of the repressive sections of the 1922 Act. Amongst other measures, the Emergency Act provided for non-jury courts, arrest without warrant, interrogation without an attorney present, and internment without trial. As a consequence of the atrocities committed under these repressive Acts, the European Court of Human Rights in 1978 found the British guilty of "inhuman and degrading treatment". Amnesty International in its 1978 report on human rights found that "systematic brutality" was used in Castlereagh Police Barracks during interrogations.

The 26-County government has been just as brutal to its political dissidents as has the 6-county administration. The pro-Treaty government, at the onset of the civil war in 1922, set up military tribunals to sanction the execution of Republican prisoners of war. Also, in a blatant affront to human rights and the rules of war, they summarily executed Republican prisoners in reprisal for military attacks on their forces. Again, in 1931 the 26-County government set up a Special Powers Tribunal to silence Republican activists as they had done in 1922. Eight years later in 1939, in response to an IRA campaign in England, the 26-County government enacted the Offenses against the State Act, which as in 1922 and 1931 provided for military tribunals that again sanctioned the imprisonment and execution of Republicans. In subsequent years, the Special Powers Act was amended to circumvent the rules of evidence, impose censorship, arrest without warrant, detain incommunicado, interrogate without an attorney present, and incarcerate without trial political and civil rights activists and others whom the government wanted silenced. As a result, the 26-County government was criticized and reprimanded by the European Court of Human Rights for the use of such repressive measures against its citizens, a reprimand they choose to ignore.

Separation of Church and State

The Separation of Church and State is essential for achieving a just and lasting peace in Ireland and is central to Éire Nua. The lessons of history require that. Ireland today is a multi-cultural, pluralistic society that must cater equally to all its citizens irrespective of their religious affiliations. Religious freedom will be protected under the Éire Nua constitution. Organized religion will be free to propagate and grow and the individual will be free to join or remain apart. Religion will not dabble in politics nor will the government use religion to advance their political agendas.

Since organized religion was first established, the relationship between Church and State has been uneasy, if not downright contentious. These relations first became a serious problem in the latter days of the Roman Empire when Christianity became the State religion. As the authority of the Roman Empire waned, Popes took over the universal authority of the Emperor's and the Episcopal Hierarchy filled the void of collapsing Imperial Administrations. When the Roman Empire finally collapsed, the Christian Church took its place and nearly all of Europe's rulers submitted to its power and authority.

At the height of papal supremacy in the Middle Ages, Pope Boniface VIII, who reigned from 1294 to 1203, issued a papal decree declaring that the pope should have a voice in civil as well as religious affairs. This decree angered civil authorities. In reprisal, King Philip of France used his influence to have a French archbishop elected to succeed

Boniface VIII. The new Pope, Clement V, moved the papal residence to Avignon in France and appointed only French cardinals. The now polarized Papacy remained in France during the reign of seven French popes. The seeds of dissension sown during this period set in motion a series of divisive events culmination in the Great Schism of the West. The Schism, which lasted for forty years, resulted in competing popes and cardinals, who were supported and used by feuding European rules to further their own particular agendas. The ensuing abuse and misuse of ecclesiastical powers led to the Reformation of 1517, a revolution within the Roman Church that gave birth to Protestantism.

The quest for power and supremacy between the Church of Rome and the civil authorities in Europe was felt in Ireland. The Reformation divided the Christian church and pitted the countries of Europe against each other. As the consequence of a rift between King Henry VIII and Pope Clement VII over the question of supremacy, Protestantism became the state religion in England. Remaining true to their beliefs, the Irish people sided with the Church of Rome.

After the defeat of the Catholic armies at the battles of the Boyne and Aughrin in 1690, the English enacted a series of repressive anti-Catholic laws. These laws, collectively known as the Penal Laws, deprived Catholics of their religious freedom, political, and property rights. Catholic colleges were closed and priests were not allowed to attend to their flock. Property owners who refused to convert to Protestantism were classified as disloyal and summarily dispossessed of their lands. Protestant settlers were brought in from Scotland and England and given the lands and possessions taken from the native Irish property owners. Religion became a powerful weapon to suppress the Irish people and formed the basis for the *"divide & rule"* doctrine used by the English down through the centuries to rule and control the Irish people.

After the Reform Act of 1850, which modified the Penal Laws, the new face of the Catholic Church was romanistic, authoritarian, and determined to enter the political arena to protect its vested interests. Its attitude towards Irish nationalism was adversarial in that it had to compete for the loyalty of the populace. Although some priests were sympathetic and at times joined in the struggle for independence, the hierarchy did not consider Irish independence important or desirable. As repayment to the English for establishing Maynooth College, a seminary for priests, the hierarchy vehemently condemned resistance to English rule. The Church entered the political arena to ensure the downfall of Parnell, who posed a constitutional threat to the English. To weaken resistance to English rule they summarily excommunicated all those who took part in the uprisings of 1867 and 1916. They also condemned anti-Treaty forces during the civil war of 1922. To this very day they condemn those who engage in anti-British activities.

An Independent Judiciary

The Éire Nua (New Ireland) proposal includes as one of its fundamental principles, an independent judicial system. The reason for this is to prevent abuses of governmental powers, common to the present system. Over the years since British rule ended, successive Irish governments have adopted repressive legislation to silence protest and political dissent. The present-day Supreme Court has been reluctant to subject such legislation to judicial review; in fact, it has been supportive and a willing party to its implementation.

The Supreme Court would be vested with the judicial power of the nation. The Court would be the final interpreter of the meaning of the Constitution, and as such would exercise the power of judicial review to ensure that legislation and/or the exercise of executive powers would not violate the Constitution. In order to ensure the independence of the Supreme Court under the Éire Nua proposal, the Court would have equal status to the legislative and executive branches of government

As head of an independent judicial system, the Court would be the ultimate tribunal in the nations court system. Within the framework of litigation, the Court would mark the boundaries of authority between the national, provincial, and local levels of government, and between the government and the citizen. Nominees to the Supreme Court would be selected by the President and confirmed by the national parliament, Dáil Éireann. The term of office for Supreme Court justices would be to mandatory retirement age, unless they are removed from office for cause. Removal from office for cause would be by a two-thirds vote of Dáil Éireann.

Appeal Courts would be established at the national level and in each of the provinces to review criminal and civil cases appealed from lower courts, or courts of original jurisdiction. Each of the Courts would consist of at least three sitting judges, to hear and rule on appeals with respect to points of law and rules of evidence.

Nominees to the Court operating at the national level would be selected by the President and confirmed by Dáil Éireann. Nominees to the Courts operating at the provincial level would be selected by Provincial

Administrators and confirmed by the provincial parliament. The term of office for Appeal Courts judges would be to mandatory retirement age, unless they are removed from office for cause. In that case judges operating at the national level would be removed from office by a two-thirds vote of Dáil Éireann and judges operating at the provincial level would be removed from office by a two-thirds vote of their respective provincial parliament.

The Central Court system would consist of a Central Criminal Court and an Administrative Court and would be established at the national level. The Central Criminal Court would be the court of original jurisdiction for cases involving civil rights, sedition, extradition, and official corruption. The Administrative Court would rule on issues of administrative law such as consumer protection, taxation, currency, trade and commerce, environmental protection, and public safety.

Nominees to the Central Court system would be nominated by the President and confirmed by the Dáil Éireann. The term of office for judges would be until they reach mandatory retirement age, unless they are removed from office for cause. Removal from office for cause would be by a two-thirds vote of Dáil Éireann.

The Circuit Court system would consist of courts of original jurisdiction operating at the provincial level for criminal, civil, and family court cases. In order to bring the judicial system close to the people, courts would be set-up in each of the provinces regions. All cases brought before these courts, with the exception of family court cases, would be tried before a jury of peers.

Nominees to the Circuit Court system would be selected by the Provincial Administrators and confirmed by the respective provincial parliament. The term of office for

Circuit Court judges would extend to mandatory retirement age, unless they are removed from office for cause. Removal from office for cause would be two-thirds vote of their respective provincial parliament.

District Courts would be established at the district level to handle misdemeanor cases, such as traffic and ordinance violations, punishable by fines and/or loss of driving privileges. These courts would be presided over by magistrates appointed to office by local councils to predetermined terms.

New Government Structures

The proposed government structures will embody a system of power sharing administered at the national, provincial, regional, and district government levels. This system will ensure maximum distribution of government powers and will accommodate the unique and distinctive character of each of the historic provinces. In addition to the above advantages, it grants autonomy to each of the provinces to pursue interests for which they have a natural affinity including cultural, traditional, and economic interests.

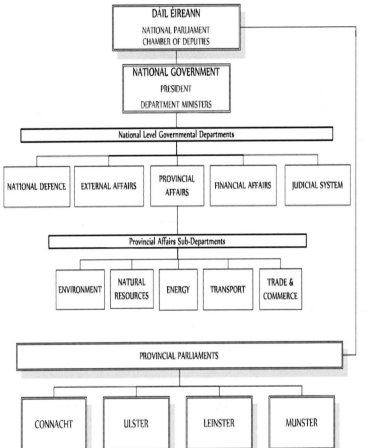

DÁIL ÉIREANN
NATIONAL PARLIAMENT
CHAMBER OF DEPUTIES

NATIONAL GOVERNMENT
PRESIDENT
DEPARTMENT MINISTERS

National Level Governmental Departments

| NATIONAL DEFENCE | EXTERNAL AFFAIRS | PROVINCIAL AFFAIRS | FINANCIAL AFFAIRS | JUDICIAL SYSTEM |

Provincial Affairs Sub-Departments

| ENVIRONMENT | NATURAL RESOURCES | ENERGY | TRANSPORT | TRADE & COMMERCE |

PROVINCIAL PARLIAMENTS

| CONNACHT | ULSTER | LEINSTER | MUNSTER |

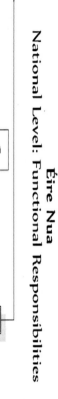

Éire Nua
National Level: Functional Responsibilities

The National Government

Éire Nua (New Ireland) will have a national parliament, Dáil Éireann, to which all citizens will give common allegiance. It will embody the unity and sovereignty of the nation as a whole. It will be the supreme national authority, acting in trust for the people with a special duty to uphold the constitution and protect the national interests at home and abroad.

Dáil Éireann will be a federal parliament in that it will be drawn from the federation of Ireland's four constituent provinces. It will consist of a single chamber of deputies, 50% elected by direct universal suffrage and 50% in equal numbers from each provincial parliament. Their actions will be governed by the constitution. The federal parliament will be responsible for electing a President who will serve as both prime minister and head of state, confirm government ministers nominated by the President, initiate and enact legislation, and approve the national budget.

The national administration will manage the affairs of state, as mandated by national legislation. It will do so through its governmental departments. As administrative responsibilities will reside with different levels of government, the national government's authority will be limited to those affairs that reside at the national level, including defense, external affairs, financial affairs, and the judicial system.

Éire Nua
Provincial Level: Functional Responsibilities

DÁIL ÉIREANN
NATIONAL PARLIAMENT
PROVINCIAL PARLIAMENT
CHAMBER OF DEPUTIES
PROVINCIAL GOVERNMENT
CHIEF ADMINISTRATOR
DEPARTMENT ADMINISTRATORS
Provincial Level Government Departments
NATURAL RESOURCES & ENVIRONMENT
ENERGY & COMMUNICATIONS
REGIONAL COORDINATION
3RD LEVEL EDUCATION & CULTURAL AFFAIRS
TRADE & COMMERCE

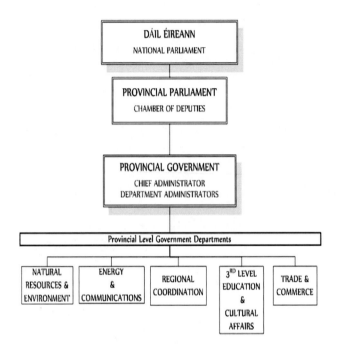

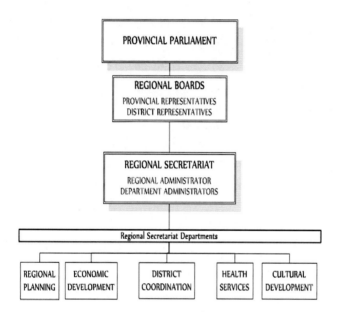

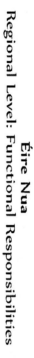

PROVINCIAL PARLIAMENT

REGIONAL BOARDS
PROVINCIAL REPRESENTATIVES
DISTRICT REPRESENTATIVES

REGIONAL SECRETARIAT
REGIONAL ADMINISTRATOR
DEPARTMENT ADMINISTRATORS

Regional Secretariat Departments

REGIONAL PLANNING

ECONOMIC DEVELOPMENT

DISTRICT COORDINATION

HEALTH SERVICES

CULTURAL DEVELOPMENT

Provincial Governments

Provincial Parliaments will be established in each of the provinces. These parliaments will each consist of a single chamber of deputies whose members will be elected by the people of the provinces. Their actions will be governed by the constitution. The function of these parliaments will be to draft rules and regulations to implement legislative mandates, elect members to represent the province in Dáil Éireann, elect a provincial administration, initiate legislation, and approve the provincial budget.

Provincial Administrations will be responsible for managing provincial government affairs including natural resources, the environment, energy and communications, trade and commerce, third-level education, and cultural affairs.

Regional Boards will be established in each of the provinces. The Boards will be comprised of elected representatives of district councils and expert representatives appointed by the provincial parliament. Regional Boards will be responsible for economic development, regional planning, regionalized health services, and cultural development.

Local Governments

District/county Councils will be established in each district/county. Each council will consist of a single chamber of representatives elected by the people of the district/county. Local Councils will be responsible for drafting rules and regulations to implement legislative mandates, and for approving the district budget. Their actions will be governed by the constitution.

District/county Administrators will be responsible for managing local government affairs including law enforcement, employment and work standards, welfare and social services, primary and secondary education, agriculture and fisheries, primary health care, recreation, the environment, public safety, and public housing.

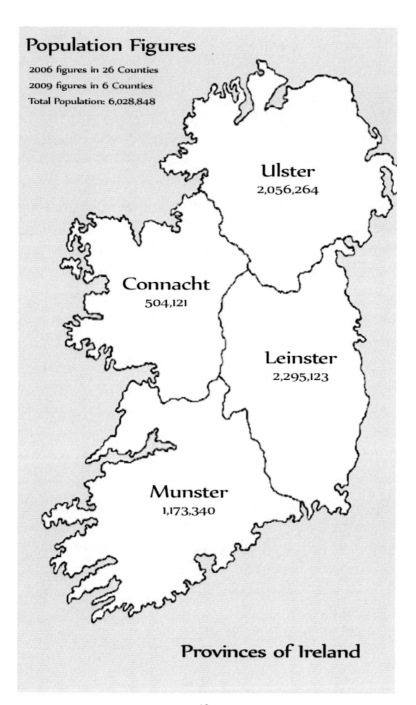

Population Figures

2006 figures in 26 Counties
2009 figures in 6 Counties
Total Population: 6,028,848

Ulster
2,056,264

Connacht
504,121

Leinster
2,295,123

Munster
1,173,340

Provinces of Ireland

A Brief Note on Emigration

While numbers would seem to indicate that emigration has been curtailed, the truth of the matter is that the increased population has come from immigration of new residents from nations recently joining the European Union. Native Irish emigration rates, therefore, cannot necessarily be seen in the population figures directly.

We can use the following mathematical formula to extrapolate a rough statistic of emigration in Ireland:

$$\frac{(26\ \text{County Emigrants} + 6\ \text{County Emigrants})}{(26\ \text{County Population} + 6\ \text{County Population})}$$

Therefore, we arrive at:

$$\frac{(27{,}700^{8} + 11{,}200^{9})}{(4{,}239{,}848^{10} + 1{,}789{,}000^{11})}$$

or

38,900 / 6,028,848 = .006 emigrants / per capita (approx.)

---

8 CSO; "Population and Migration Estimates April 2010" (only native Irish emigration figure used)

9 NISRA; "Migration Statistics for Northern Ireland 2009"; November 2010

10 CSO; "Principal Statistics: Population of each Province, County and City, 2006"

11 NISRA; "The Population of Northern Ireland"

In lay man's terms, that means at the current rate of emigration roughly 1 out of every 200 native Irish citizens, inclusive of the whole island, can be expected to feel compelled to leave their nation behind due to economic, social, or political inequity.

Similarly, this formula can be used to extrapolate emigration rates as targeted as one can obtain data for, even down to specific towns were such figures at hand.

A Geopolitical View of Éire Nua

National Capital
Athlone
Provincial Capitals
Ulster - Dungannon
Connacht - Tuam
Leinster - Dublin
Munster - Cork

WEST ULSTER
BELFAST
DUNGANNON
GRT. BELFAST
ULSTER
EAST ULSTER
SOUTH ULSTER
NORTH CONNACHT
CONNACHT
MIDLANDS
DUBLIN
GRT. DUBLIN
TUAM
SOUTH CONNACHT
ATHLONE
LEINSTER
EAST LEINSTER
NORTH MUNSTER
SOUTH LEINSTER
MUNSTER
EAST MUNSTER
SOUTH MUNSTER
GRT. CORK
CORK

An overview of the Provinces

The Provinces

CONNACHT

Region I -- North Connacht consisting of Sligo, Leitrim, North Mayo, and North Roscommon.

Region 2 -- South Connacht consisting of Galway, South Roscommon, and South Mayo

MUNSTER

Region I -- Cork City and environs.

Region 2 -- South Munster consisting of Kerry and North and West Cork.

Region 3 -- East Munster consisting of South Tipperary, Waterford, and East Cork.

Region 4 -- North Munster, consisting of North Tipperary, Limerick, and Clare.

LEINSTER

Region I -- Greater Dublin.

Region 2 -- Midlands consisting of Longford, Westmeath, Laois, and Offaly.

Region 3 -- East Leinster consisting of South Louth, Meath, Kildare, and Wicklow.

Region 4 -- South Leinster, consisting of Wexford, Carlow, and Kilkenny.

ULSTER

Region I Greater Belfast.

Region 2 -- East Ulster consisting of Antrim, East Derry, East Tyrone, North Armagh, and North and East Down.

Region 3 -- South Ulster consisting of Cavan, Monaghan, South Fermanagh, South Down, South Armagh, and North Louth.

Region 4 -- West Ulster consisting of Donegal, West Derry, West Tyrone, and North Fermanagh.

Connacht

Cúige Connacht

"remote, beautiful, Connacht,
viewed today much as it was
in the invader Cromwell's time...."

Connacht is the smallest in area and population of the four historic provinces of Ireland. It is situated in the west of Ireland between the North Atlantic (to the west) and the Shannon River (to the east). Historically, it has been neglected; in the first instance by the British occupiers and later by the 26-County government. Economically, it is the least developed province and consequently has experienced the greatest loss of its youth to emigration. Connacht is home to the Gaelic-speaking people of Ireland, with the exception of other small pockets in Kerry and Donegal.

Within the Éire Nua concept, Connacht would have its own Parliament, seated in Tuam, the capital. The parliament would consist of a single chamber of deputies elected by the people of the province according to a system of proportional representation. The function of the parliament would be to:

1. coordinate cultural activity and economic development within its regions,

2. initiate and promote legislation for the social, economic, and cultural development of its people,

3. coordinate the development and expansion of third-level education, and

4. collect provincial taxes.

In order to maximize the concept of devolved government, Connacht would include within its geographical boundary two clearly defined economic regions, North Connacht and South Connacht. Each region would be administered by a regional board consisting of:

1. representatives of district councils from within the region, and

2. expert representatives appointed by the provincial parliament.

These regional boards would be responsible for establishing, promoting, and coordinating their own social, economic, and cultural programs.

Within each region, ten clearly defined districts would be established. Each district would be administered by a district council, covering a population of between 10,000 and 40,000 people. District councils would be responsible for

1. law enforcement and the administration of justice,

2. primary and secondary education,

3. public works and local planning,

4. welfare and social services, and

5. recreational development.

Voluntary Community Councils would be established at the local level to pursue local issues.

Munster

Cúige Mumhan

"fertile, gentle, Munster..."

Munster is surrounded by Connacht to the north, Leinster to the east and by the Atlantic Ocean to the south and west. It covers an area of 9,550 sq. miles and has a population of 1,173,340[12]. Munster has fared much better economically than Connacht, due primarily to:

1. 80% of the land in Munster is arable compared to less than 50% in Connacht,

2. land holdings in Munster are much larger than those in Connacht, and

3. Munster is home to the Irish dairy industry, which has up to now provided the home-grown economic base sorely lacking in Connacht, and for that matter, in the rest of Ireland.

It has a population density of 123 per sq. mile, compared to Connacht with a density of 76 per sq. mile and Leinster with a density of 301 per sq. mile.

Within the Éire Nua concept, Munster's parliament would be seated in Cork, the capital. The parliament would consist of a single chamber of deputies elected by the people of the province according to a system of proportional representation. The function of the parliament would be to:

1. coordinate cultural activity and economic development within its regions,

2. initiate and promote legislation for the social, economic, and cultural development of its people,

_____

12 Province population & population density have been updated throughout to reflect current numbers.

3. coordinate the development and expansion of third-level education, and collect provincial taxes.

In order to maximize the concept of devolved government, Munster would include within its geographic boundary four clearly defined regions: namely, North Munster, South Munster, East Munster, and Greater Cork. Each region would be administered by a regional board consisting of:

1. representatives of district councils from within the region, and

2. expert representatives appointed by the provincial parliament.

These boards would be responsible for administering the criminal justice system and for establishing, promoting, and coordinating their own social, economic, and cultural programs.

Within each region, clearly defined districts would be established. North Munster would have eight, South Munster nine, East Munster five, and Greater Cork two. Each district, which would have a population of between 10,000 and 40,000 people, would be administered by a district council. District councils will be responsible for:

1. law enforcement and the administration of justice,

2. primary and secondary education,

3. public works and local planning,

4. welfare and social services, and

5. recreational development.

Voluntary community councils will be established at the local level to pursue local-level issues.

Ulster

Cúige Uladh

"rebellious, rugged Ulster..."

Ulster is situated in the northern part of Ireland. It is surrounded by the Atlantic Ocean on the north and west and by the Irish Sea on the east. It covers an area of approximately 9,000 square miles and has a population of 1,737,000. Six of the nine counties are presently occupied and controlled by the British army. Ulster is home to the Protestant Irish and is the main battleground in the present phase of the struggle for Irish freedom. In the New Ireland, Ulster would be the first province to have its own parliament.

Within the Éire Nua concept, Ulster's parliament would be seated in Dungannon, the capital. The parliament would consist of a single chamber of deputies elected by the people of the province according to a system of proportional representation. The function of the parliament would be to:

1. coordinate cultural activity and economic development within its regions,

2. initiate and promote legislation for the social, economic, and cultural development of its people,

3. coordinate the development and expansion of third-level education and collect provincial taxes.

In order to maximize the concept of devolved government, Ulster would include within its geographic boundary four clearly defined economic regions: namely, West Ulster, Greater Belfast, East Ulster and South Ulster. Each region would be administered by a regional board consisting of:

1. representatives of district councils from within the region, and

2. expert representatives appointed by the provincial parliament.

These regional boards would be responsible for administering the criminal justice system and for establishing, promoting, and coordinating their own social, economic, and cultural programs.

Within each region, clearly defined districts would be established. West Ulster would have ten districts, Greater Belfast would have one, East Ulster would have fourteen, and South Ulster would have seven. Each district would be administered by a district council, covering a population of between 10,000 and 40,000 people. District councils would be responsible for

1. law enforcement and the administration of justice,

2. primary and secondary education,

3. public works and local planning,

4. welfare and social services, and

5. recreational development.

Voluntary Community Councils would be established at the local level to pursue local issues.

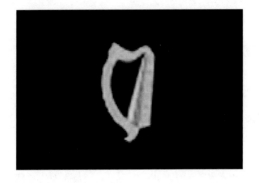

Leinster

Cúige Laighean

"rich Leinster, the center of the Pale..."

Leinster is situated in the eastern part of Ireland. It is surrounded by Connacht and Munster to the west, Ulster to the north, the Irish Sea to the east and the Atlantic Ocean to the south. It covers an area of 7,618 square miles and has a population of 2,295,123. Generally, Leinster has fared better economically than the other provinces, primarily because Dublin, the historic center of power and influence in Ireland, is located within its boundaries. It is the most densely populated province with a population density of 301 per square mile, compared to Connacht with a density of 76 per square mile.

Within the Éire Nua concept, Leinster's parliament would be seated in Dublin, the capital. The parliament would consist of a single chamber of deputies elected by the people of the province according to a system of proportional representation. The function of the parliament would be to:

1. coordinate cultural activity and economic development within its regions,

2. initiate and promote legislation for the social, economic and cultural development of its people,

3. coordinate the development and expansion of third-level education, and

4. collect provincial taxes.

In order to maximize the concept of devolved government, Leinster would include within its geographic boundary four clearly defined regions, namely, the Midlands, South Leinster, East Leinster, and Greater Dublin. Each region would be administered by a regional board consisting of:

1. representatives of district councils from within the region, and

2. expert representatives appointed by the provincial parliament.

These regional boards would be responsible for administering the criminal justice system and for establishing, promoting, and coordinating their own social, economic, and cultural programs.

Within each region, clearly defined districts would be established. The Midlands would have six, South Leinster would have six , East Leinster would have seven, and Greater Dublin would have thirty-two. Each district, which would have a population of between 10,000 and 40,000 people, would be administered by a district council. District councils would be responsible for:

1. law enforcement and the administration of justice,

2. primary and secondary education,

3. public works and local planning,

4. welfare and social services, and

5. recreational development.

Voluntary Community Councils would be established at the local level to pursue local issues.

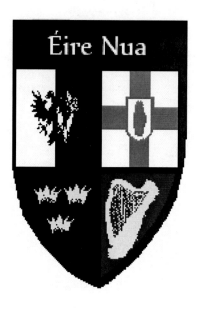

An early emblem used to promote the Éire Nua program

The Religious Traditions in Ireland[13]

The Birth of Protestantism

The Reformation of 1517, a religious revolution begun within the Catholic Church by a German monk named Martin Luther to protest the sale of titles, indulgences, and other practices of the Church, gave birth to Protestantism. Its influence had a profound effect on the social, political, and economic life of Europe and on Ireland in particular. Within 40 years, it had divided Europe between the Protestant countries of the north and the Catholic countries of the south. By 1534 it had spread to England. As the result of a rift between Pope Clement VII and King Henry VIII over the question of supremacy, Anglicanism, a form of Protestantism headed by the monarch, replaced Catholicism as the official state religion of England. During this period other forms of Protestantism were being established, differing mainly in their system of control. In Scotland, John Knox established the Presbyterian Church, a form of Protestantism based on the teachings of John Calvin. In 1560 it became the state religion of Scotland.

Protestantism's Spread to Ireland

In 1541 Henry VIII declared himself king of Ireland and started what came to be known as the Tudor conquest of Ireland. He also introduced Protestantism to Ireland. During his reign and that of his successors, the Tudor conquest of Ireland continued. Eventually, most of the

13 Originally serialized in *Éire Nua Newsletter Vol. 2, #2* & *Vol. 2, #3* as "The Protestant Tradition in Ireland" & "The Catholic Tradition in Ireland".

Irish landlords submitted to his will, converted to Protestantism and swore allegiance to him. They did so, in order to hold on to their lands. The only exceptions were the Ulster landlords who, instead of submitting, intensified their resistance to English rule. In 1593, they engaged in the first of a series of revolts which collectively became known as the Nine Year War. These revolts ended in 1603 at the battle of Kinsale. Irish forces led by Hugh O'Neill were defeated. Four years later, unwilling and unable to accept defeat, O'Neill with ninety other leading Ulstermen went into exile in Europe. This "flight of the Earls" left the people of Ulster leaderless, and presented King James I with the perfect opportunity to solve once and for all the problem of Ireland's chief trouble spot, Ulster. He expelled most of the Catholics from there, seized their land and gave it to English and Scottish settlers. The subjugation of Ulster and the Tudor conquest of Ireland was complete.

Protestantism in a New Ireland

On the role of Irish Protestants in a new Ireland the following excerpts are taken from the 1992 Easter Commemoration Address by Judge John Collins of the New York Supreme Court at Gaelic Park in New York sums it up best:

"It is unfortunate that the Protestant majority in the north looks to England for their protection, and I am convinced that that is why they look to England. Other than that, they have no particular love for England. They are Irish people with a distinct tradition. Irish people of the Catholic tradition, whether north or south of the border, are not seeking to obliterate the traditions of the Irish Protestant. It will be a fortunate day for Ireland when the two traditions are combined in one nation, for the Protestants of the north will bring to one nation a proud, noble, and hardworking people, who will contribute in a beneficial way to Ireland's

economy. They will bring to a government a distinctly new and different flavor, all to the good."

A Common Homeland

As we open the second decade of a new millennium, it is incumbent on the Irish people, irrespective of their ancestry or religious affiliation, to reassert their control over the political process and charter a new course for Ireland. They must embrace new political models, such as Éire Nua, to ensure a better life for themselves and secure a future for their children. The politicians who are now in control are busy pursuing policies conducive to another plantation of sorts, this time by outsiders occupying the vacant homes and farms of Irish people forced to emigrate. Provisions of the Common Market Treaty, which came into effect this year, allow for the free movement of people across borders. In Germany these people will be migrant workers, in Ireland they will be the new landlords. People of both traditions in Ireland must work together to preserve what is theirs by tradition and birthright, a common homeland.

The Birth of Catholicism

As the old pagan Roman Empire decayed, there grew up in its midst a new spiritual empire, the Roman Catholic Church. In the course of time replaced the Roman Empire in Western Europe and carried on the Roman tradition of unity in administration, law, language, and culture. When the Roman Empire finally collapsed and disappeared, the Roman Catholic Church was prepared to take its place. The popes took over the universal authority of the emperors, and the episcopal hierarchy filled the void left by the withdrawal of the imperial administration. The unity of the Roman Catholic Church was the bond that held the people of Western Europe together throughout the chaotic centuries of the Middle Ages. These events of so long ago were to have a major impact on the course of Irish history.

Catholicism in Ireland

Contrary to popular belief, there were Christians in Ireland before St. Patrick arrived. Trading with Roman Britain and Gaul saw to that. Some scholars from Gaul may even have sought refuge in Ireland during the Germanic invasion of the Roman Empire. In any case, Christians were sufficiently numerous by the year 431 to justify the appointment of Palladius by Pope Clementine as the first bishop of the Irish who believed in Christ.

As a result of popular legend and Patrick's own writings, his reputation as the apostle of Ireland obscured those of his contemporaries. Even so, his impact was indeed considerable. His main achievement, however, was his ability to inspire a great many fervent followers, who together with their successors completed the conversion of Ireland and extended their influence throughout Britain and Europe.

Ireland's Golden Age

For the next 400 years the Catholic Church flourished in Ireland. Over 800 monasteries and fifty large churches were founded. Many of the monasteries had an international reputation for piety and learning. The great masterpieces of illuminated manuscripts, including the Book of Kells and the Book of Durrow, were produced during this period. Irish monastic expansion reached as far afield as England, France, Germany, Belgium, Switzerland, Italy, and Austria. This indeed was Ireland's golden age when peace and tranquility reigned and Ireland was free.

Catholicism and Repression

By the time of the first Viking raids in 795 the early fervor of the monastic movement was in decline. Fewer monasteries were founded and many of the existing ones were destroyed by the Vikings. By the time of the Norman invasion in 1169, there were few monasteries left. During the fourteenth century there were a few brief revival movements inspired by the introduction of Augustinian and Cistercian monks to Ireland. The monastic life resumed its decline during the fifteenth century, succumbing to poverty and spiritual decline.

In 1534, when Henry VIII became *Supreme Head on Earth of the Church of Ireland*, the real political and religious repression of the Irish people began. The penal laws and land confiscation which followed deprived the Catholic population of their religious freedom and livelihood. By the year 1870, the population of Ireland was decimated by famine and emigration and only 3% of the land was owned by Catholics. Since then, conditions have improved for the majority of Ireland's Catholics.

Catholicism in a New Ireland

Both states in Ireland discriminate against their minorities. The 26-county State prevents non-Catholics from following their consciences in such matters as divorce and contraception. The 6-county State openly and blatantly discriminates against Catholics in politics, employment, education, and housing.

In the New Ireland, with its constitutional guarantees of equal rights and opportunity for all its citizens, religion will no longer play a part in the affairs of state. The separation of Church and State will guarantee the various denominations the freedom to attend to the spiritual needs of their adherents. By the same token, the Government will not be in the business of legislating morality. Instead, it will cater to the temporal needs of all its citizens including Catholics, Protestants, Jews, and non-believers alike who make up the entire population.

Éire Nua & The 26-County State[14]

The Government of Ireland Act, enacted by the British Parliament in 1920 and ratified by the Anglo-Irish Treaty of 1921, divided Ireland into two dominion states of the British Empire; the 26-county Irish "Free State" and the "Northern Ireland State". This Act not only divided Ireland; it divided its people. As was mentioned earlier, the Anglo-Irish Treaty was the most insidious of all the tragedies perpetrated on the Irish people. In effect, it denied the people of the Catholic and Protestant traditions the opportunity to work together to build a nation in which they could both prosper and live in peace. What it did instead was to perpetuate British control and create a climate for self-serving politicians in both states to enrich themselves at the people's expense.

The "Northern Ireland State" includes the six northeastern counties of Ireland: Antrim, Down, Armagh, Tyrone, Fermanagh, and Derry. It covers an area of 5,400 square miles, approximately 17% of the whole island's area. It has a population of 1,789,000[15] which is about 30% of the total island population. The inclusion of six counties in the make-up of the new state instead of the nine historic

---

14 Originally appeared in *Éire Nua Newsletter Vol. 2, #1* as as "Ireland's Political Dilemma" & *Vol. 3, #1* as "Ireland's Hidden Agenda".

15 Population figures quoted are from 2009 NISRA & 2006 26-County information. The figures, as of 1993 when this was first written, were listed as 1,528,000 and 35% of the total population. Scholars should note the increase is primarily due to immigration from Europe which managed to meet and exceed native Irish emigration levels. The Six County statelet actually rose to 1,923,251 in 1998, experiencing a sharp decline afterwards followed by moderate growth, NI State estimates indicate that the population growth of the Six Counties is, despite predictions of growth in 2010, now stalling and on the cusp of reversing.

counties of Ulster was the option favored by the Unionists because it gave them the greatest possible majority: 78% to 22% in a six county state versus 52% to 48% in a nine county state. Prior to 1972, when the British reestablished direct control, the "Northern Ireland State" was governed by self-professed bigots who openly discriminated against the nationalist population.

The 26-county state includes the remaining counties. It covers an area of 27,136 square miles and has a population of 4,239,848[16]. In 1948, the Dublin Parliament enacted the Republic of Ireland Act wherein the the 26-county Free State ceased to be a British dominion. Since it's creation in 1922, the 26-county state has been governed by political families whose primary goal was, and still is, to hold on to power at any cost in order to protect their own privileged lifestyles. Although power passed back and forth between political families and parties in the interim, the primary goal did not change; the status quo prevailed, the governing elite grew richer, and emigration, the system's built-in safety valve, continued to export Ireland's greatest resource: its youth. Ireland, with its youth, would indeed have threatened the status quo.

The consequences of the ill-conceived Government of Ireland Act and the attendant Anglo-Irish Treaty can be measured in terms of their effect on Irish society. The most immediate effect is the ongoing war and the loss of over 3,000 lives since 1969. Secondly, the stagnant Irish economy which depends on bailouts and handouts from the EEC has spawned one of the highest unemployment rates in Europe. This, in turn, has fueled emigration to the point where it has become a way of life for the youth of

---

16 Again, based on 2006 figures. The original figures listed, as of 1993, were 3,670,000. Current 26-county demographic numbers indicate a migration to the cities, possibly symptomatic of the implosion of the "Celtic Tiger".

Ireland. Finally, in a blatant affront to civil rights, authorities in both states use special government powers to silence their critics. The methods used include surveillance by special police and military units, arrest without warrant, and imprisonment for extended periods without trial. In those cases where an individual is brought to trial, it is generally before a military or a non-jury court where the state desired verdict is rendered 99% of the time.

The Old Paradigm

Government representatives who engage in periodic peace initiatives to end the war in the occupied six counties represent only the interests of the political and economic elite in London, Dublin, and Belfast. Unfortunately for the people of Ireland, their interests matter little and have never been a factor in any of the ensuing discussions. It's doubtful if the sponsors of these initiatives consider, or for that matter care, what's best for the Irish people.

Among the positions represented in these discussion, the British government's position is the most difficult to understand.

They act as if the empire still exists and that their continuing presence in Ireland is critical to its survival. It's clear from the lessons of history that their presence is not linked to the welfare of the Irish people, be it Catholic or Protestant, as they have never demonstrated anything other than contempt for the Irish.

It's much easier to understand the twenty-six county government's position. The system has been and continues to be very profitable for the political families who have ruled there since 1922. Many of the leading politicians have become wealthy while in office as a result of patronage and influence peddling. They owe their positions of power and privilege to the partition of Ireland and as a consequence only pay lip service to Irish unity. They have a major stake in maintaining the status quo.

The Belfast politicians on the other hand have openly practiced their own form of corruption and graft. Some Unionist leaders have preached hate in the name of God to divide people and create a climate in which their brand of politics flourishes. They have done this effectively and enriched themselves in the process. Whenever their political existence is threatened they survive by becoming "proxy Brits" and playing the orange card. While pontificating about peace, Nationalist politicians have also benefited by working for the British and drawing multiple salaries in the process.

There is little hope of a solution emerging from any of these so-called peace initiatives, as the aim of the players is the preservation of the status quo. In the meantime the people, particularly the youth, suffer the consequences. They endure the ever present scourge of unemployment and emigration, which together have become a national disease, pervasive and gnawing at the soul of the Irish psyche. The same old players, the same old cards, the same old paradigm equals the status quo.

The New Paradigm

Recognizing that the sponsors of the aforementioned initiatives have a vested interest in the status quo, Republican Sinn Féin has proposed the Éire Nua program as a fair and comprehensive plan for achieving a just and lasting peace in Ireland. The authors consider this program to be innovative and worthy of promotion in the United States. The authors further believe it to be a positive initiative which recognizes the rights of all Irish people, irrespective of their ancestry or religious affiliations.

The Éire Nua program, first authored by the late Dáithí Ó Conaill, is visionary in concept and far reaching in that it includes all of Ireland. It offers a solution that guarantees equality and the maximum distribution of authority at provincial and subsidiary levels in a unitary federal system comprising the historic four provinces of Ireland. It views the war in the North as an ongoing effort to remove the last vestiges of colonialism and not as a conflict between Ireland's Catholics and Protestants. It sets forth specific conditions to start the process of reconciliation and unity including:

1. a British declaration of intent to withdraw from Ireland,

2. the release of all political prisoners,

3. the convening of a constitutional convention to draft a new all-Ireland constitution.

   The greatest obstacle faced by proponents of this plan is the lack of access to the media in Ireland and England which is under government control in both countries. The Irish people can be trusted to choose what's best for Ireland, if given the facts and opportunity to do so. Under these circumstances, it would not be presumptuous to believe that the people would support a settlement that they were allowed to consider and approve.

   This is the new challenge for those of us who believe in a new beginning for Ireland. We must understand the problems we face and from that understanding work for a just solution.

THE IRISH CRISIS

HON. THOMAS P. O'NEILL, JR.
OF MASSACHUSETTS

IN THE HOUSE OF REPRESENTATIVES
Thursday, June 28, 1973

Mr. O'NEILL. Mr. Speaker, Mr. Fred Burns O'Brien has compiled a group of materials proposing a solution to the present situation in Northern Ireland which merits consideration. As a frequent visitor to the North, and a student of the political and social developments which has created the crisis in Northern Ireland, Mr. O'Brien speaks with considerable knowledge of the subject. I am placing in the record a collection of pieces, edited with an introduction by Mr. O'Brien, which outline at least one approach to resolving the tragic crisis which has been plaguing Northern Ireland for many years:

REGIONALISM: A SOLUTION TO
THE IRISH CRISIS

(Edited by Fred Burns O'Brien)

INTRODUCTION

The events in Northeast Ireland over the past four years have been particularly tragic in Ireland's incessant struggle to attain self-determination for her people. The present conflict could best be curtailed with the implementation of a system of government for the entire island that would be conducive to the interests of the various Irish communities that will be vying for power. A system must be created that would cater to the loyalists that predominate in the Six Counties known to the world as Northern Ireland as well as the aspirations of nationalists who are in the minority.

Such a system does exist and has been given scrutiny by politicians in the North who are diversely opposed on most issues. This system is based on a federal approach similar to that of the United States and it will provide for a gracious amount of autonomy for the four historic regions of Ireland.

THE REGIONAL STRUCTURE
(By Ruiari O'Bradaigh)

The object of the Republican movement is to establish a new society in Ireland—EIRE NUA. To achieve that aim, the existing system of undemocratic Partition rule must be abolished and replaced with an entirely new system based upon the unity and sovereignty of the Irish people.

A NEW CONSTITUTION

The New Constitution would provide:
(a) A charter of rights which would incorporate the principle of securing to the individual protective control of his conditions of living subject to the common good.
(b) A structure of government which would apply this principle by providing for the maximum distribution of authority at provincial and subsidiary level.

FEDERAL GOVERNMENT

1. The Federal Parliament, Dail Eireann, would be a single chamber of approximately 150 deputies elected as follows:
(a) fifty per cent by direct universal suffrage on the Proportional Representation system.
(b) fifty per cent in equal numbers from each central parliament
2. The Federal Parliament would control all powers and functions essential to the good of the whole nation.
3. The Federal Parliament would elect a President who would be both Prime Minister and Head of State.
4. The President would nominate a Government consisting of a limited number of ministers for election by the Federal Parliament.
5. Members elected to the Government would relinquish their seats in the Federal Parliament. There would be a provision for electing a restricted proportion of the Government from outside Dail Eireann.
6. The independence of the Supreme Court and judicial system, as the guardian of the Constitution would be secured.
7. National legislation would be initiated by any of the following agencies:
(a) Federal Parliament deputies
(b) The Central Government
(c) A Provincial Parliament
(d) Referendum
8. National legislation would be adopted by:
(a) Federal Parliament
(b) Referendum in specified cases

PROVINCIAL GOVERNMENT

Four democratically elected Provincial Parliaments (Dail Uladh, Dail Laighean, Dail Chonnacht and Dail na Mumhan) based on the four historic provinces of Ireland—Ulster, Leinster, Connacht, and Munster—would deal with their respective areas.

The establishment of Dail Uladh would be the first step towards the creation of this new government structure for the whole island. By thus creating a Provincial Parliament for the nine counties of Ulster within a New Ireland, the partition system would be disestablished and the problem of the border removed. Dail Uladh would be representative of Catholic and Protestant, Orange and Green, Left and Right. It would be an Ulster Parliament for the Ulster people. The Unionist-oriented people of Ulster would have a working majority within the Province and would therefore have considerable control over their own affairs. That power would be the surest guarantee of their civil and religious liberties within a New Ireland.

REGIONAL GOVERNMENT (ADMINISTRATION)

Regional Development Councils would be established to promote and co-ordinate the economic, social and cultural affairs of clearly defined economic regions. For example, East Ulster and West Ulster, having different economic problems, would require separate Regional Development Councils.

The Regional Development Council would be a single chamber consisting of:
(a) Representatives of Community Councils within the region concerned
(b) A commission of experts appointed by the Provincial Government

COMMUNITY GOVERNMENT (LOCAL)

A system of Community Government would replace the existing local government authorities North and South. It would consist of Community Councils democratically elected by the people on a Proportional Representation basis. A Council would govern an area which has physical and social unity, and on the basis of justice and efficiency would take and implement decisions appropriate to its area, with the minimum control by Central Government, in accordance with the principle of subsidiarity of function. In brief, a Community Council would be a local people's assembly. Councils would vary in size and area of jurisdiction. In determining a Council area of jurisdiction, physical and social unity would be the principal factors along with the wishes of the local inhabitants.

(img courtesy: Fred Burns O'Brien)

Due largely to the efforts of Fred Burns O'Brien & others, a synopsis of the Eire Nua program was entered into the Congressional Record in 1973[17].

---

17 Congressional Record of the 93rd Congress: First Session Volume 119, Number 103; Friday June 29, 1973 in the Extension of Remarks.

A Draft Charter of Rights

We, the people of Ireland, are resolved to establish political sovereignty, to secure human justice and social progress in this island, to achieve a better life for all, and henceforth to live in peace with one another. And so we declare our adherence to the following principles:

- Article 1. Every citizen is born free and equal and shares the same inherent human dignity. Everyone is entitled to the rights of citizenship without distinction as to race, sex religion, philosophical conviction, language, or political outlook.
- Article 2. Every citizen has the right to life, liberty, and security of person. No-one shall be subjected to arbitrary arrest of detention.
- Article 3. Every citizen has the right to freedom of conscience, to free choice and practice of religion, and to the free and open teaching of ethical and political beliefs. This includes the rights to freedom of assembly, the right to peaceable association, the right to petition, and the right to freedom of expression and communication.
- Article 4. Every citizen has the right to participate in the government of the country, and to equal access to its public service.
- Article 5. The basis of government is the will of the people. This is expressed in direct participatory democracy and free elections by secret ballot. The right of every citizen to follow his or her conscience, and to express his or her personal opinion, stands against any demographically contrived attempt at repression.

- Article 6. Every citizen has the right to education according to personal ability, the right to work, and the right to a standard of living worthy of a free human being. This right extends to food, housing and medical care, and to security against unemployment, illness, and disability.
- Article 7. Every citizen has the right to marry and found a family. Mothers, children, the aged, and infirm deserve the nation's particular care and attention.
- Article 8. Every citizen has the right to equal pay for equal work, and the right to join a trade union for the protection of workers' collective interests, and these rights must be acknowledged by all employers.
- Article 9. In the exercise of their rights, citizens shall be subject only to such constraints as may be necessary to ensure recognition and respect for the rights of others and the welfare of the larger community.

Political Documents of the Irish Republic 1916-1919

From a fundamental Irish Republican viewpoint, there are four primary documents from which to draw on as the blueprint for the legitimate all-Irish Republic proclaimed in 1916. Careful attention to these documents as well as the Éire Nua program will reveal many similarities. The structure of Éire Nua is designed to meet the standards of the non-sectarian all-Irish Republic. This unique attribute lends Éire Nua a legitimacy and credibility sorely lacking in current and past British and 26-County alternatives.

In this light we include the following documents as an appendix: The Proclamation of the Irish Republic, The Declaration of Independence, The Democratic Programme, and A Message to the Free Nations of the World.

The 1916 Proclamation of the Irish Republic

POBLACHT NA H-ÉIREANN
THE PROVISIONAL GOVERNMENT
OF THE IRISH REPUBLIC
TO THE PEOPLE OF IRELAND

IRISHMEN AND IRISHWOMEN: In the name of God and of the dead generations from which she receives her old tradition of nationhood, Ireland, through us summons her children to her flag and strikes for her freedom.

Having organised and trained her manhood through her secret revolutionary organisation, the Irish Republican Brotherhood, and through her open military organisations, the Irish Volunteers and the Irish Citizen Army, having patiently perfected her discipline, having resolutely waited for the right moment to reveal itself, she now seizes that moment, and supported by her exiled children in America and by gallant allies in Europe, but relying in the first on her own strength, she strikes in full confidence of victory.

We declare the right of the people of Ireland to the ownership of Ireland, and to the unfettered control of Irish destinies, to be sovereign and indefeasible. The long usurpation of that right by a foreign people and government has not extinguished the right, nor can it ever be extinguished except by the destruction of the Irish people. In every generation the Irish people have asserted their right to national freedom and sovereignty; six times during the past three hundred years they have asserted it in arms. Standing on that fundamental right and again asserting it in arms in the face of the world, we hereby proclaim the Irish Republic as a Sovereign Independent

State, and we pledge our lives and the lives of our comrades-in-arms to the cause of its freedom, of its welfare, and of its exaltation among the nations.

The Irish Republic is entitled to, and hereby claims, the allegiance of every Irishman and Irishwoman. The Irish Republic guarantees religious and civil liberty, equal rights and equal opportunities to all its citizens, and declares its resolve to pursue the happiness and prosperity of the whole nation and all of its parts, cherishing all the children of the nation equally, and oblivious of the differences carefully fostered by an alien Government, which have divided a minority from the majority in the past.

Until our arms have brought the opportune moment for the establishment of a permanent National Government, representative of the whole people of Ireland and elected by the suffrages of all her men and women, the Provisional Government, hereby constituted, will administer the civil and military affairs of the Republic in trust for the people.

We place the cause of the Irish Republic under the protection of the Most High God, Whose blessing we invoke upon our arms, and we pray that no one who serves that cause will dishonour it by cowardice, inhumanity, or rapine. In this supreme hour the Irish Nation must, by its valour and discipline and the readiness of its children to sacrifice themselves for the common good, prove itself worthy of the august destiny to which it is called.

Signed on behalf of the Provisional Government

Tomás Ó Cléirigh
Seán Mac Diarmada   Tomás Mac Donncha
Pádraig Mac Piarais   Seosamh Pluincéad
Séamas Ó Conghaile   Eamonn Ceannt

Message To the Free Nations of the World[18]

To the Nations of the World—Greeting

The Nation of Ireland having proclaimed her national independence, calls, through her elected representatives in Parliament assembled in the Irish Capital on January 21st, 1919, upon every free nation to support the Irish Republic by recognising Ireland's national status and her right to its vindication at the Peace Congress.

Naturally, the race, the language, the customs and traditions of Ireland are radically distinct from the English. Ireland is one of the most ancient nations in Europe, and she has preserved her national integrity, vigorous and intact, through seven centuries of foreign oppression; she has never relinquished her national rights, and throughout the long era of English usurpation she has in every generation defiantly proclaimed her inalienable right of nationhood down to her last glorious resort to arms in 1916.

Internationally, Ireland is the gateway to the Atlantic; Ireland is the last outpost of Europe towards the West; Ireland is the point upon which great trade routes between East and West converge; her independence is demanded by the Freedom of the Seas; her great harbours must be open to all nations, instead of being the monopoly of England. To-day these harbours are empty and idle solely because English policy is determined to retain Ireland as a barren bulwark for English aggrandisement, and the unique geographical position of this island, far from being a benefit

18 Issued at the first meeting of the first (All-Ireland) Dáil Éireann January 21, 1919

and safeguard to Europe and America, is subjected to the purposes of England's policy of world domination.

Ireland to-day reasserts her historic nationhood the more confidently before the new world emerging from the war, because she believes in freedom and justice as the fundamental principles of international law; because she believes in a frank co-operation between the peoples for equal rights against the vested privileges of ancient tyrannies; because the permanent peace of Europe can never be secured by perpetuating military dominion for the profit of empire but only by establishing the control of government in every land upon the basis of the free will of a free people, and the existing state of war, between Ireland and England, can never be ended until Ireland is definitely evacuated by the armed forces of England.

For these among other reasons, Ireland—resolutely and irrevocably determined at the dawn of the promised era of self-determination and liberty that she will suffer foreign dominion no longer—calls upon every free nation to uphold her national claim to complete independence as an Irish Republic against the arrogant pretensions of England founded in fraud and sustained only by an overwhelming military occupation, and demands to be confronted publicly with England at the Congress of the Nations, that the civilised world having judged between English wrong and Irish right may guarantee to Ireland its permanent support for the maintenance of her national independence.

Declaration of Independence[19]

Whereas the Irish People is by right a free people:

And Whereas for seven hundred years the Irish people has never ceased to repudiate and has repeatedly protested in arms against foreign usurpation.

And Whereas English rule in this country is, and always has been, based upon force and fraud and maintained by military occupation against the declared will of the people:

And Whereas the Irish Republic was proclaimed in Dublin on Easter Monday, 1916, by the Irish Republican Army acting on behalf of the Irish people:

And Whereas the Irish people is resolved to secure and maintain its complete independence in order to promote the common weal, to re-establish justice, to provide for future defence, to insure peace at home and goodwill with all nations and to constitute a national policy based upon the people's will with equal right and equal opportunity for every citizen:

And Whereas at the threshold of a new era in history the Irish electorate has in the General Election of December, 1918, seized the first occasion to declare by an overwhelming majority its firm allegiance to the Irish Republic:

Now, therefore, we, the elected Representatives of the ancient Irish people in National Parliament assembled, do,

19 Issued at the first meeting of the first (All-Ireland) Dáil Éireann January 21, 1919

in the name of the Irish nation, ratify the establishment of the Irish Republic and pledge ourselves and our people to make this declaration effective by every means at our command:

We ordain that the elected Representatives of the Irish people alone have power to make laws binding on the people of Ireland, and that the Irish parliament is the only parliament to which that people will give its allegiance:

We solemnly declare foreign government in Ireland to be an invasion of our national right which we will never tolerate, and we demand the evacuation of our country by the English Garrison:

We claim for our national independence the recognition and support of every free nation in the world, and we proclaim that independence to be a condition precedent to international peace hereafter

In the name of the Irish people we humbly commit our destiny to Almighty God who gave our fathers the courage and determination to persevere through long centuries of a ruthless tyranny, and strong in the justice of the cause which they have handed down to us, we ask His divine blessing on this the last stage of the struggle we have pledged ourselves to carry through to Freedom.

The Democratic Programme of Dáil Éireann[20]

We declare in the words of the Irish Republican Proclamation the right of the people of Ireland to the ownership of Ireland, and to the unfettered control of Irish destinies to be indefeasible, and in the language of our first President. Pádraig Mac Phiarais, we declare that the Nation's sovereignty extends not only to all men and women of the Nation, but to all its material possessions, the Nation's soil and all its resources, all the wealth and all the wealth-producing processes within the Nation, and with him we reaffirm that all right to private property must be subordinated to the public right and welfare.

We declare that we desire our country to be ruled in accordance with the principles of Liberty, Equality, and Justice for all, which alone can secure permanence of Government in the willing adhesion of the people.

We affirm the duty of every man and woman to give allegiance and service to the Commonwealth, and declare it is the duty of the Nation to assure that every citizen shall have opportunity to spend his or her strength and faculties in the service of the people. In return for willing service, we, in the name of the Republic, declare the right of every citizen to an adequate share of the produce of the Nation's labour.

It shall be the first duty of the Government of the Republic to make provision for the physical, mental and spiritual well-being of the children, to secure that no child

20 Issued at the first meeting of the first (All-Ireland) Dáil Éireann January 21, 1919

shall suffer hunger or cold from lack of food, clothing, or shelter, but that all shall be provided with the means and facilities requisite for their proper education and training as Citizens of a Free and Gaelic Ireland.

The Irish Republic fully realises the necessity of abolishing the present odious, degrading and foreign Poor Law System, substituting therefor a sympathetic native scheme for the care of the Nation's aged and infirm, who shall not be regarded as a burden, but rather entitled to the Nation's gratitude and consideration. Likewise it shall be the duty of the Republic to take such measures as will safeguard the health of the people and ensure the physical as well as the moral well-being of the Nation.

It shall be our duty to promote the development of the Nation's resources, to increase the productivity of its soil, to exploit its mineral deposits, peat bogs, and fisheries, its waterways and harbours, in the interests and for the benefit of the Irish people.

It shall be the duty of the Republic to adopt all measures necessary for the recreation and invigoration of our Industries, and to ensure their being developed on the most beneficial and progressive co-operative and industrial lines. With the adoption of an extensive Irish Consular Service, trade with foreign Nations shall be revived on terms of mutual advantage and goodwill, and while undertaking the organisation of the Nation's trade, import and export, it shall be the duty of the Republic to prevent the shipment from Ireland of food and other necessaries until the wants of the Irish people are fully satisfied and the future provided for.

It shall also devolve upon the National Government to seek co-operation of the Governments of other countries in determining a standard of Social and Industrial

Legislation with a view to a general and lasting improvement in the conditions under which the working classes live and labour.

Cumann Na Saoirse Náisiúnta
Position Paper

The Éire Nua program, initially proposed by Republican Sinn Féin in 1972, would as a basic requirement, reunite the British occupied six counties of Ireland with the rest of Ireland in an all-Ireland federation comprised of the four historic provinces of Ulster, Munster, Leinster and Connacht. This comprehensive and far-reaching program is in stark contrast to British imposed arrangements such as the Anglo-Irish Treaty of 1921, Sunningdale, Hillsborough, and the Good Friday Agreement, all calculated to copper-fasten and legitimize British control over the occupied six counties of Ireland.

The British imposed Government of Ireland Act of 1920, coupled with the Anglo-Irish Treaty of 1921, partitioned the Irish nation into two dominion states of the British Empire, the 26-county Free State and the occupied 6-county administration. This British enforced arrangement was the most insidious of all the treacherous acts perpetrated on the Irish nation, it not only divided Ireland; it also divided its people. As a consequence, it denied the people of different religions and traditions the opportunity to work together to build a nation in which they both could prosper and live in peace. Instead, as intended this insidious arrangement perpetuated direct British control over the occupied six counties and indirect control over the twenty-six county state.

Any political program that does not include the reunification of the Irish nation as a prerequisite is meaningless and doomed to failure from the start.

The Éire Nua program authored by the late Dáithí Ó Conaill, Ruairí Ó Brádaigh and others is visionary in concept and far reaching in that it includes all of Ireland. It offers a solution that guarantees equality and the maximum distribution of authority at provincial and subsidiary levels in a unitary federal system comprising the four provinces of Ireland. It views the war in the North not as a religious conflict but as an ongoing effort to remove the last vestiges of colonialism. It sets forth specific conditions to start the process of reconciliation and unity including;

A British declaration of intent to withdraw from Ireland,

The convening of a constitutional convention to draft a new all-Ireland constitution

The unconditional release of all political prisoners, and a British withdrawal.

The proposed all-Ireland constitution embodies the following fundamental principles,

A Charter of Rights that would clearly define the rights and privileges to be accorded to each and every individual.

New Governments Structures that would embody a system of power sharing administered at the national, provincial, county / district government levels.

The Separation of Church and State would guarantee the various religious denominations the freedom to attend to the spiritual needs of their adherents. By the same token, the government would not be in the business of legislating morality.

An Independent Judiciary that would ensure that the nations' Supreme Court, as guardian of the constitution, would have equal status to the legislative and executive branches of government. The judicial power of the nation would be vested in the Supreme Court.

The NIFC consider the Éire Nua program to be innovative and far-reaching and believes it to be a positive approach that recognizes the rights of all Irish people, irrespective of their ancestry or religious affiliations. For this reason the NIFC has adopted and will promote Éire Nua as the most logical choice to achieve a lasting peace for Ireland. We believe that this program is based on sound and honorable principles incorporating fair and realistic plans to achieve national unity within the framework of a 32-county Irish Republic.

Bibliography & Suggested Reading

Population Figures:

- NISRA; "A Demographic Portrait of Northern Ireland"; *Population Trends* 135 (Spring 2009)

- NISRA; "Migration Statistics for Northern Ireland 2009"; November 2010

- Central Statistics Office; "Principal Statistics: Population of each Province, County and City, 2006"

Éire Nua & Related Thought:

- White, R. *Ruairí Ó Brádaigh: The Life and Politics of an Irish Revolutionary.* Bloomington: University of Indiana Press, 2006.

- Fennel, D. *Take the Faroes for Example.* Dublin: Pobol Teoranta, 1972.

- Fennel, D. *A New Nationalism For The New Ireland.* Monaghan: Comhairle Uladh, 1972.

- Fennel, D. *Sketches of the New Ireland.* Galway: Association for the Advancement of Self-Government, 1973.

- O'Connel, E. *The Consequences of Monetary Union.* Dublin: Common Market Study Group, 1972.

- O'Connel, E. *Dáil Uladh: Shaping A New Society.* unlisted: n/p, 1973.

- Ó Brádaigh, R. *Our People, Our Future.* Dublin: Sinn Féin, 1973.

- *Éire Nua – A New Democracy.* Dublin: Republican Sinn Féin, 2000.

- *Towards A Peaceful Ireland.* Dublin: Republican Sinn Féin, 1991.

- *Éire Nua Newsletter* (Vol. 1, #1 through Vol. 3, #1). Parlin: Eire Nua, Inc., 1991-1994.

- *A Decade of Deceit.* New York: Irish Northern Aid, 1981.

- *The Quality of Life in the New Ireland.* Dublin: Sinn Féin, 1979.

- *The National Offshore.* Dublin: Sinn Féin, 1977.

- Bairéid agus Ó Murcada. *Focus: The Irish Question.* Bronx: Irish Northern Aid, 1975.

- *Peace with Justice*. Dublin: Sinn Féin, 1972.
- *Mining and Energy*. Dublin: Sinn Féin, 1974.
- *Agriculture – the need for planned development*. Dublin: Sinn Féin, undated.
- *Women in the New Ireland*. Unlisted, undated: Sinn Féin.

Irish-American Activism:
- O'Reilly, D. (Editor). *Accepting the Challenge: The Memoirs of Michael Flannery*. Dublin: Irish Freedom Press, 2001.
- O'Dowd, N. *Periscope: "Emmett O'Connell – A Prophet Before His Time"*. *http://www.irishcentral.com/story/news/periscope/emmett-oconnell-a-prophet-before-his-time-111586514.html* – Last Accessed 11 May 2012.

Irish Civil Rights Struggle:
- Wilson, D. *An End to Silence*. Cork: Royal Carbery Books, 1990.
- Clarke, Sis. Sarah. *No Faith in the System: A Search for Justice*. Cork & Dublin: Mercier Press, 1995.

The Éire Nua Campaign in the United States

Éire Nua (New Ireland) is a comprehensive Irish authored political program designed to achieve a just and lasting peace in Ireland in the context of a British withdrawal. Initially proposed by Sinn Féin in 1972, Éire Nua sets forth specific proposals to start the process of Irish reunification and reconciliation. It also includes proposals for a new all-Ireland constitution. The principle on which Éire Nua is based envisions a system of government in which all creeds and traditions would be represented and all citizens could exercise real power, without any one group infringing on the right of others.

Objectives

1. To increase awareness in the U.S. of the Irish authored Éire Nua political program and the proposals contained therein to achieve a just and lasting peace in Ireland in the context of a British withdrawal from the occupied six counties

2. To engage political leaders, the media and the American public in bringing pressure to bear on the U.S. government to reverse its selective visa denial policy directed at Éire Nua proponents.

Associated Activities

1. Prepare information packages for general distribution containing information relevant to the campaign.

2. Conduct Éire Nua related seminars and presentations at colleges, other institutions, and private parties.

3. Petition government bodies, institutions and organizations to pass resolutions supporting Éire

Nua as a viable alternative to the Good Friday Agreement

4. Lobby legislators to initiate hearings on government's policy that denies entry visas to Éire Nua proponents.

5. Conduct a letter-writing campaign targeting newspapers and politicians and other interested parties regarding Éire Nua and competing proposals and the denial of visas to Éire Nua proponents

Participating in the Campaign

1. Hand out Éire Nua related flyers and other promotional materials to friends and other interested parties when an opportunity presents itself.

2. Gather signatures on petitions relating to the denial of visas by the U.S. government to Éire Nua proponents to visit the U.S. for the purpose of promoting Éire Nua.

3. Join with other members and supporters in a letter-writing campaign.

Contact the National Éire Nua Campaign Committee
at eirenuavisa@irishfreedom.net

or at the postal address shown below for additional information on how to help

National Irish Freedom Committee

P.O. Box 358

Bronx, NY 10470

USA